MATTHEW ANTEZZO
DOPPELPUNKT

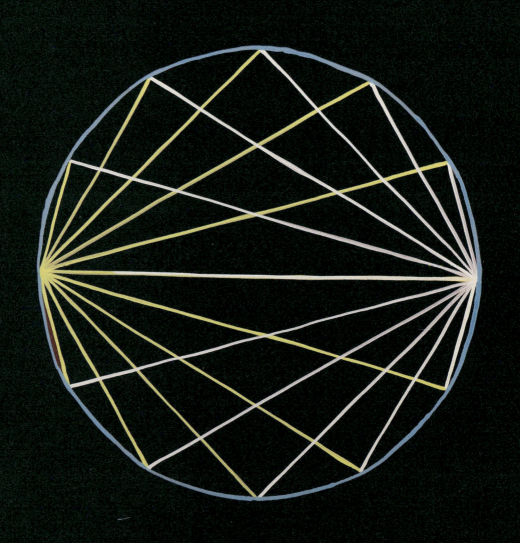

MATTHEW ANTEZZO
DOPPELPUNKT

Stefan,
Always electric.
with love

FROM GÖTTINGEN TO THE MOON

Often I wonder at things that are taken for granted: elevators, watches which take the wearer's temperature, cordless telephones, GPS navigators.

They're all black boxes. We can see the effect of information going in and information going out, but, if we have to say how they work ... well, I'm not sure many of us could.

These things were once the fantasies found in comic books: television-watches, handheld video communication devices, talking computers. Now that we have all this stuff, it's hard to imagine a time when we didn't. It brings us to a state of instant access to everything, everywhere, but what's underneath it? Sure, we can understand how it works, but how is it affecting us?

What happened?
For many years I was concerned with this question as a starting point for art making. Recently the question has shifted to: what happens when ... [fill in the blank]?

After being invited to make this exhibition, I found out that the Mathematics Institute at the University of Göttingen has a model collection.
The institute's building was designed with the collection as a central feature so that the students would pass through and see these objects every day.

Later, talking with a physicist about his work on material structures – phenomenon on the level of the invisible – it became apparent how the language of these phenomena is full of metaphor, observation is through equipment, and ideas surrounding these things are like shadows on the wall.

This may seem rather obscure and unconnected, but, if one looks, the lines may become clearer. With this exhibition, I took some works, which represent a long time period, and put them together in a way that could make some of these connections relate in ways which vibrate and illuminate.

It seems almost quaint 40 years later: Neil Armstrong, climbing down a ladder to the surface of the moon.
How did we get there?
I know a good route via Göttingen.

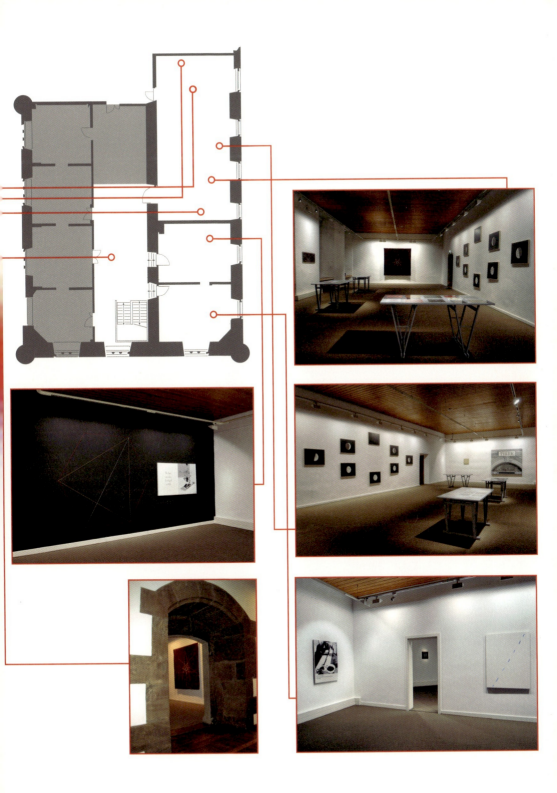

4. *Evening News. Alan Turing. The Enigma,*
   2002, pencil and graphite on paper, diptych, 23 x 61 cm

5. *T.I.M.,*
   2008, gouache on cotton twill, 40 x 40 cm

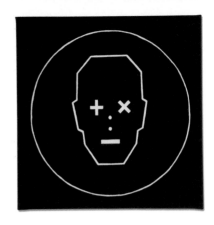

'ELECTRONIC' ATHLETE

Antithesis of the popular notion of a scientist is tall, modest, 34-year-old bachelor Alan M. Turing, scratch man in the Walton Athletics Club's three-mile open event on Boxing Day. Turing is the club's star distance runner, although this is his first season in competitive events. At the National Physical Laboratory, at Molesey [sic], he is known as Dr Turing, [and] is also credited with the original idea for the Automatic Computing Engine, popularly known as the Electronic Brain. He is diffident about his prowess in science and athletics, gives credit for the donkey work on the ACE to Americans, says he runs only to keep fit, but admits he rowed in his college eight at Cambridge.

Mind over Body

over Mind

TIM, TIME IS MONEY

Alan Turing also designed the Bombe, the cryptanalytic machine used to simulate the rotors of the Enigma machine.

David Hilbert

While Chairman of Mathematics at at U. of Göttingen, Hilbert proposed a set of problems; one being the "Entscheidungsproblem" which asked for an algorithm which would give a "True" or "False" answer to any mathematical statement.

The allies won WWII having cracked the German code machine the "Enigma".

It was Alan Turing's work on building the method and machines to break the code which in large part made for their success.

ab

"Enigma cryptography machine".

ac

Alan Turing

In 1936 while working on the "Entscheidungsproblem" Turing concieved the theoretical basis for the modern computer.

His work later became crucial in the challenge of code breaking during the war.

A.T. was a world-class long distance runner.

'ELECTRONIC' ATHLETE

Antithesis of the popular notion of a scientist is tall, modest, 34-year-old bachelor Alan M. Turing, scratch man in the Walton Athletics Club's three-mile open event on Boxing Day. Turing is the club's star distance runner, although this is his first season in competitive events. At the National Physical Laboratory, at Molesey [sic], he is known as Dr Turing, [and] is also credited with the original idea for the Automatic Computing Engine, popularly known as the Electronic Brain. He is diffident about his prowess in science and athletics, gives credit for the donkey work on the ACE to Americans, says he runs only to keep fit, but admits he rowed in his college eight at Cambridge.

1

Even though he was an important stratigic asset, Turing was "chemically castrated" for the crime of a homosexual act. This punishment which he chose over imprisonment, changed his body to such a degree that it is thought he chose suicide to end his life in 1953.

6. *History of Computing, home. t-online.de/home/horst.zuse/show.html (Konrad Zuse)*
   1999, oil on canvas, diptych, 76 x 61 cm and 16 x 83 cm

Konrad Zuse

Elegance in

In 1936, computer pioneer Konrad Zuse, a civil engineer from Germany, built (in the living room of his parents' house in Berlin,) the Z1, the first mechanical binary computer. In 1941, despite financial hardship and isolation from computer scientists from other Western countries, Zuse created the world's first programmable computer, the Z3, from spare telephone parts.

ba

bb

His Z3 computer was the world's first working programmable, fully automatic computing machine; whose attributes, have often been the ones used as criteria in defining a computer. The Z3 uses 2,000 relays (an electric switch) and was used to design aircraft. Calculations on the computer were performed in full binary floating point arithmetic.

The Z3 read programs off punched film. In addition to his technical work, Zuse founded one of the earliest computer businesses in 1946. This company built the Z4, which became

Konrad Zuse

the Architecture

the second commercial computer leased to the Swiss Institute of Technology in Zürich, 1950.

Due to World War II, however, Zuse's work largely unnoticed in the UK and the U.S.

Zuse also suggested that the universe itself is running on a grid of computers (digital physics); he published the book Rechnender Raum (translated into English as Calculating Space).

punched film

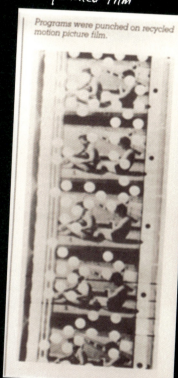

Programs were punched on recycled motion picture film.

7. *Bell labs* II
   1999, oil on linen, diptych, 91 x 152 cm

The first transistor, developed in 1948.

Early console radios

Families gathered to listen.

First application of transistor for consumer use were in hearing aids

I pod shuffle, listening device capable of holding hundreds of hours of music.

Before transistors, electronic circuits used glass tubes and were very unreliable.

Transistorized portable radios allowed individuals the freedom to listen away from the group, changing the social structures and causing cultural changes such as Rock-n-Roll to flourish.

A Monument to

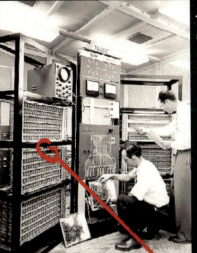

TRADIC at Bell Labs. Early transistorized computer

— PARADIGM SHIFT —

The first transistor, developed in 1948.

A transistor is a semiconductor device which can either switch or amplify electronic signals. This simple invention led to the miniaturization of all electronic devices.

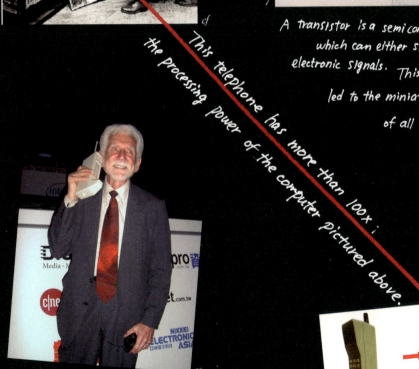

This telephone has more than 100x the processing power of the computer pictured above.

Martin Cooper, inventor of the mobile telephone.

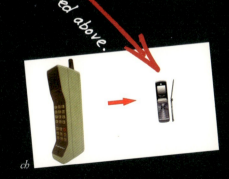

Miniaturization

8. *Nam June Paik, Video Time, Video Space, (Edition Cantz, 1991), p. 31*,
   1999, oil on linen, diptych, 107 x 71 cm

Zen for Head 1962
Fluxus Internationale Festspiele Neuester Musik,
Wiesbaden

Zen For Head

da

Nam June Paik, the playful father of video art. His presence was in many places in post war art. Composing, Fluxus, Video Art, Media Art, Sculpture, Performance.

Other artists made similar gestures, Paul McCarthy, "Face Painting" performance, he pushes a bucket of paint with his head. Janine Antoni, "Tender Loving Care", a work where she mops the floor with her hair dye using her head.

Zen for Head 1962
Fluxus Internationale Festspiele Neuester Musik, Wiesbaden

Sony "Portopack", first portable video system

db

Paik's relation to technology
was long and ahead of the pack.
He was interested in networks
and tapping into the
latest satellite broadcast techniques
long before the internet
was available.
All the while keeping the
playful Flux-attitude.

dc

ea. web of anxiety
   1991, acrylic on canvas, 66 x 81 cm

9. *Deep Cover*
   1991, acrylic on canvas, 122 x 92 cm

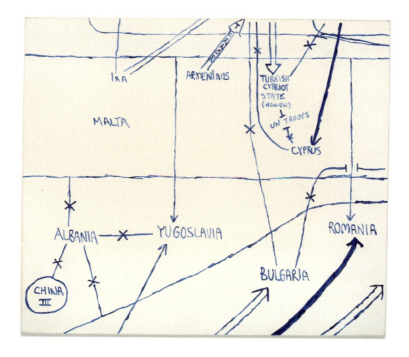

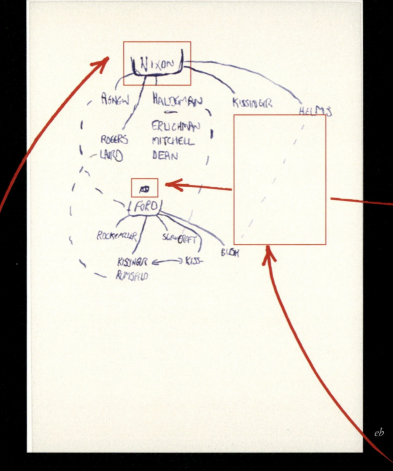

A.T.P.M. All the presidents men.

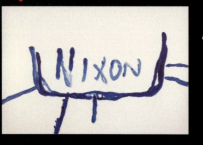

Nixon's downfall rested on his desire for total power, and he used technology (wiretapping and secret recordings) as instruments to amplify his power and manipulate the process of governing.

Power Made Abstract

Questions: What happened
And what happens?

Corruption of the highest office
of government — how?

Partially through the means
of technology. wiretapping,
secret recordings.

ed

9

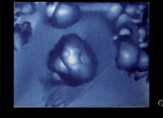
ef

Painting based on microscopic
view of ink...

Based on diagrams, these painting took a system and separated
pieces for analysis. A method to understand the parts'
relation to the whole and the hierarchies present.
On the level of painting, the question became happens when
objects are changed in scale and cropping affect meaning.

eg. M.O.T.W., (corner),
    1990, acrylic on canvas, 61 x 61 cm

eh. M.O.T.W., (box),
    1990, acrylic on canvas, 61 x 61 cm

ei. M.O.T.W.,(map of the world),
    1990, acrylic on canvas, 100 x 140 cm

 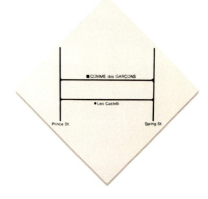

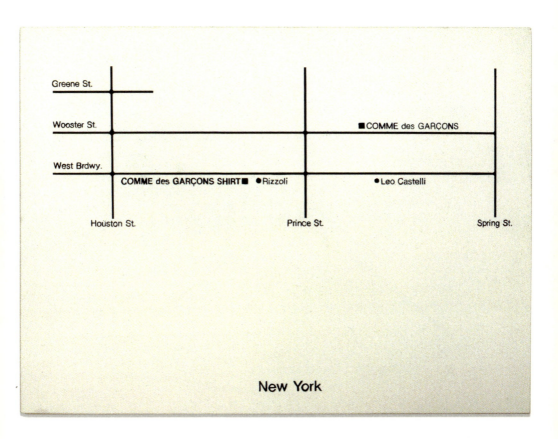

10. Mr. Fuller
   1999, oil on linen, 61 x 122 cm

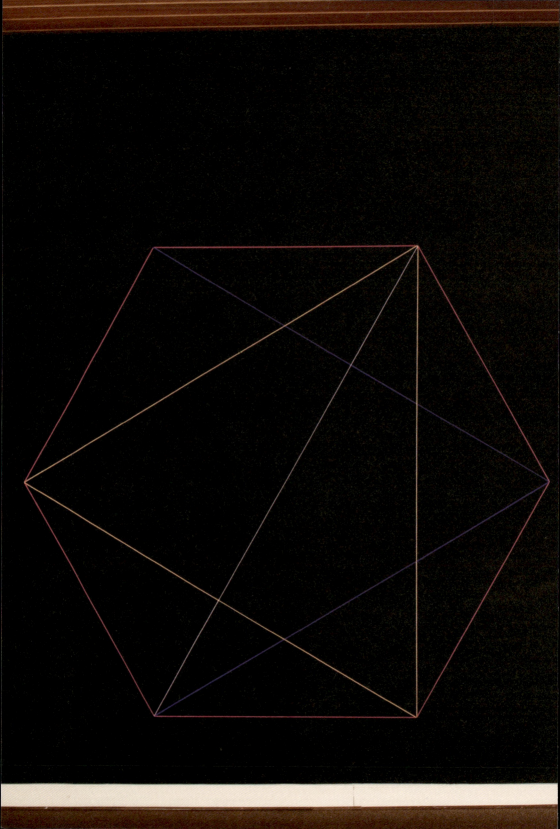

The first transistor, developed in 1948.

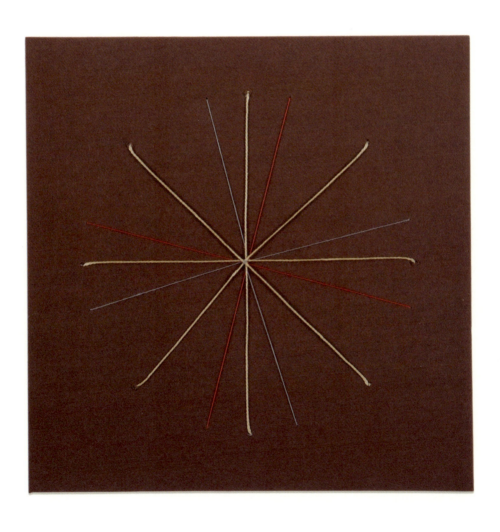

selected drawings from:

Gruppe von fünfzehn, (cf. p. 5)
2008-2010, casein on paper, 20 x 20 cm ea.

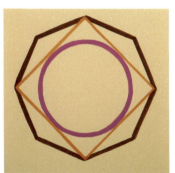

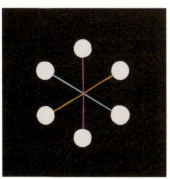
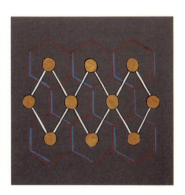

selected drawings from:

Gruppe von dreizehn, (cf. p. 5)
2008-2010, casein on paper, 20 - 30 cm ea.

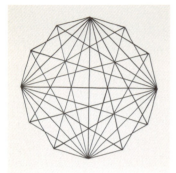

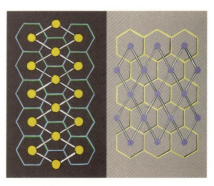
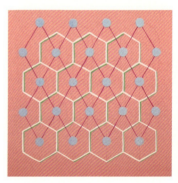

Empty it

What are devices?
How is digital logic represented?

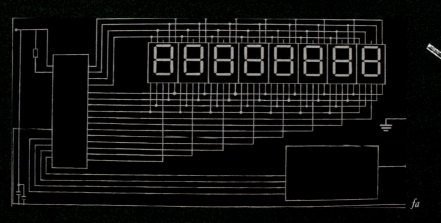

— SCHEMATICS —

Some simple devices,

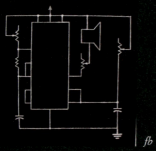

sound synthesizer,

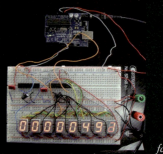

clocks, counters,

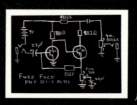

distortion pedal for guitar.

Numbers?
Play with the logic of numbers.

fe

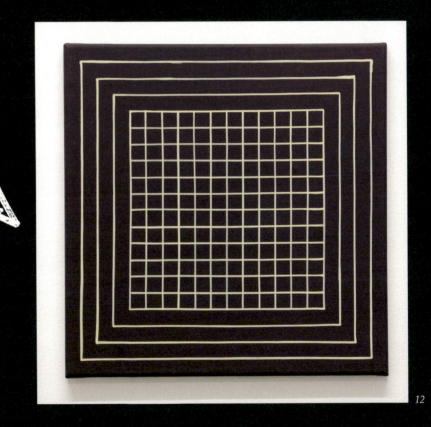

12

REMOVE THE PHYSICAL DEVICE.

What kind of devices are these?

out

Non-representational.

selected drawings from:

Gruppe von zwölf, (cf. p. 5)
2008-2010, casein on paper, 20 - 30 cm ea.

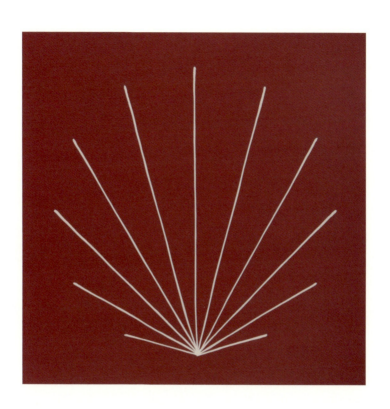

Tensile Invocations

ga

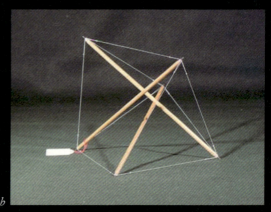
gb

Buckminster Fuller made the tensile into a lifes work.

Drawing down the stars and heavens.

gc

mauer schnur, who are you calling to?

gd

ge

if the drawings took a whole wall.?

Colored thread, wool, yarn

the project with an effecency of means?

gg. *vier, sechs, sieben K und die verbotenen Minoren,*
 2009, installation with Elise Florenty
 Künstlerhäuser Worpswede and Barkenhoff-Stiftung, Worpswede

gh. 11/12, 13/14,
    2009, colored cord, 362 x 178 cm
    installation at Klosterfelde, Berlin

ha. *http://www.ezln.org.mx*,
    2002, haute lisse, handwoven wool tapestry, 210 x 190 cm

13. *Zukunft Titel*
    2010, haute lisse, handwoven wool tapestry, 195 x 200 cm

The earliest programming techniques applied to weaving.

have been weaving the huate lisse method. each line of color is laid by hand,

Taller Mexicano

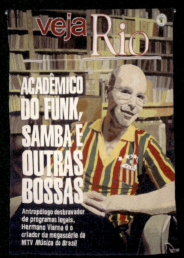

the ancient tradition of putting wool thread

dying the wool

on the loom

for over 30 years the Taller Mexicanos de Gobelinos

building the image. in a digital matrix. fully computed by the weavers

de Gobelinos

together to form the stories of today.

14. *untitled*
   2010, casien on canvas, 40 x 40 cm

15. *Tom Watson, (Think)*
   1999-2000, oil on linen, diptych, 173 x 203 cm

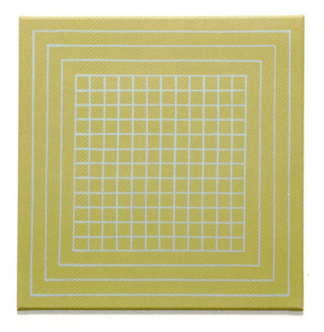

a word can give say worlds,

ia a word, loaded with meaning outside its physical presence.

a command, a statement of mission,

a request for better,

a suggestion.

Pointing to other places

Sometimes a desired destination,

ic Sometimes just somewhere else.

id

word Worlds of technology and art.

focus on language as the limits

of the physical world becomes dematerialized.

reductivist tendencies and the

drive for efficiency.

ie

Thomas Watson, Sr. of International Business Machines

realized the power

of the world think and made it

synonymous with the

company's identity

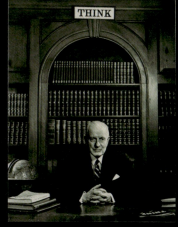
if

CONNECTING DIFFERENT DOTS

"'Well, we must wait for the future to show', said Mr. Bankes, coming in from the terrace."

It's unlikely that an artist's work should conform to the same practices and sets of interests over the course of several decades – unless it's all formal. More pertinent is the question of how a spectator might approach the sustained availability of the past in the light of a continuous present. Should old works be treated as historical or could they remain relevant other than as signifiers of development or evolution? Is it even possible for an artist to show old and new works together, without calling it a "retrospective"? Are there ways to approach the past without "looking back"? A lot of Matthew Antezzo's art, however, does seem always to have been about precisely the act of looking back – about history, about information passing through time, about knowledge becoming memory, and then, perhaps, knowledge again.

A piece like *Artforum, Nov. 1973, p. 45* (1992) appears, on the surface, to be quite dry. It's a painting whose image is a partial reproduction of a page from *Artforum*: it shows Mel Bochner's *Measurement Series Group B* from 1967. The image printed in *Artforum* shows a corner, a doorway, part of a window, and a bit of floor. Bochner measured the exhibition space and wrote the measurements on the walls of the space. The work is a classic institutional critique – involved in its entirety with drawing attention to the space in which art is presented, the white cube, and the illusion of a "neutral" gaze. Antezzo reframes the institutional critique as something to be seen hanging on a wall within a white cube. This could be read as an ironic comment on the impossibility of protest, but that would be a dry, conceptualist reading. This way of approaching the piece, however, might simply be the result of seeing it in a PDF-file or on the page of a book such as this. It's dry only on paper. Because if we consider the size of the work and the simple fact that it's a painting, something altogether more poetic starts to happen. The *Artforum*-page has been blown up to roughly 70 x 100 centimeters – many times the size of the image as it originally appeared. Should it perhaps be understood not as postmodernist critical commentary, but simply as doing what painting has so often done in its pre-modernist past: depicting something on the canvas to give it a higher status? Clearly, in this case, the work is more concerned with drawing our attention to something that's already happened: everyone knows institutional critique has, as the most important contribution to art since the 1960s, become part of the art historical canon.

It's not only that the painting gives the work a more fictionalized appearance, or puts a certain image on a pedestal in the way that a lot of painting has traditionally operated, what the work does is to highlight something else. The work isn't really about Bochner's work, but about *Artforum* – the bible of modernism – and as such about the art world itself. It becomes a comment, or lament even, on the artistic status of the institution that made Bochner's work art to begin with – the same institution that Bochner was criticizing for its ability to absorb and reconfigure – as an addition to its existing vocabulary – whatever criticism is launched at it. This is not an unusual form of commentary, though perhaps more usual in the twenty years since Antezzo's work was first made. What makes it more interesting is the stylistically "retro" look which pushes the work towards highlighting the almost romantic re-appraisal to which conceptual works and institutional critique had already been subjected by the early 90s – particularly in American publications – and similar to what had happened to the modernist work that preceded it. It's clear that the only natural response to the way modernist history was being written was to write that history itself into the artistic practice, and the result, impossible to avoid, is a certain melancholia, highlighting how nostalgia = avant-garde + time. There is no nostalgia without a prior feeling of anticipation and possibility. This is why avant-garde art eventually so easily lends itself to nostalgic feeling; nothing is more optimistic than the avant-garde, which so often represents those hopes of the past that never quite came about.

The works in which Antezzo shows famous artists as they were represented in their contemporary media, whether it's Bochner or Nam June Paik, all have this air of nostalgia about them. The imagery always looks very vulnerable. Whatever its critical qualities, avant-garde – like science – primarily deals with hope, and the idea that progress might make everything better. As such its function is nearly identical to the history of science.

The images of revolutionary leaders, scientists, and artists, all represent hope in a similar way; they are representatives of moments before we decided to give up on the idea that things evolve. The works show us residual imagery from a history that's been interpreted as finished, as if we somehow got beyond the point of no return and history itself became historical. Ultimately, however, these pieces are examples of Antezzo's personal interests and influences as an artist. They represent various stages of the artist's own path through different kinds of available material, and while this isn't where it gets interesting, these stories do add to our appreciation of the work. Perhaps the problem with the white cube was never its "falsely neutral gaze", but the way the artist is removed from their audience so that they can't talk to each other, the gallery is simply too removed from the oral tradition from which art developed, and as a result storytelling is just a little too difficult. Ideally we should always be able to go through an exhibition while having a conversation with the artist. This could make us aware, for example, that a tapestry piece like *www.ezln.org.mx*, a roughly 2 x 2 meter tapestry, was produced in Mexico by weavers who were most likely politically sympathetic to the struggles of the Zapatista movement. At the same time, the piece, as it hangs by itself, is also interesting because it involves untangling how iconic images function today. In the *www.ezln.org.mx* tapestry, for example, this happens by highlighting the strange anonymous alliance that may exist between the Internet and the life of a revolutionary guerrilla. It twists the question of what it means for something like the Zapatista movement to have become a poster campaign for anti-globalization resistance by way of online presence and representation. The tapestry takes a fully digital icon and redescribes it, without really changing it, but simply through re-presenting it within a medium that not only is wildly different

– as a medium – but which carries with it an entire medium specific history of what the originally digital icon was meant to represent. In this work Antezzo subjects digital phenomena to highly analogue treatment and presentation, much like the works where images of artists were made into paintings.

Something similar is going on in a work like *Deep Cover* (1992) where an abstract painting contains a blue dotted line diagonally across the canvas. On its own, what I personally see is blue tracks across the snow (I am, after all, from Norway), and then perhaps the slightly naïve, watercolor-like qualities of the strokes, paired with the diagonal line, could make me think the work is an ironic comment on Mondrian. The blue has a lot of white in it and is strikingly impure for an abstract painting that completely lacks expressionist qualities. Finally, there is a kind of calligraphy-like feel to it, but here too the watercolor-like quality counteracts the idea that the lines could be the result of a long process of intense pondering before carefully executing the strokes on the canvas.

So it comes as a surprise that the work is simply an enlarged close-up of a detail from a ballpoint pen diagram showing various connections between politicians, specifically between Richard Helms and George Bush Sr. – directors of the CIA under the Nixon and Ford administrations respectively. What it means, I have no idea – at least apart from how the painting ultimately becomes an example of Antezzo's interest in creating something non-representational out of a kind of highly specific historic material that so easily lends itself to all kinds of conspiracy theories and eager interpretation. Making it abstract suggests that even facts such as these, ultimately, are empty and capable of carrying whatever meaning we care to project onto them.

Images of history always involve presenting the past *as an image,* and this presentation of history as an image, as something that might be sustained and engaged with like an object, something that is readily available for repeated encounters is, partly, what a lot of these works are about. Particularly in the way that they overcompensate for the lack of stability in images that are only published digitally or in publications that disappear, or that we don't keep hold of. Magazines, in this sense, were, as a medium, definitely a precursor to the practice of Internet usage. Through the creation of images the past continues to exist in the present tense. The past is always available to us and the only question is in what manner we approach it, whether through presentation or consumption.

The works are most definitely "staged", they act and are acted upon by our seeing them, whether again or for the first time. Our understanding of the works will certainly vary with whatever order in which we happen to take them in. The sequence in which they are hung contributes to our experience, of course, but still: seeing an exhibition is never an altogether linear experience. It's a rare thing when the first work we encounter grabs hold of our attention sufficiently that we are really within it from the start. More frequently, something happens along the way, something that pulls us in, makes us invest more, and ultimately creates the context in which each of us experiences and understands the works.

As a result the works always have a presence beyond the framework set up through their individual meaning or content; there is always a meta-level of meaning that comes about through how an exhibition is mounted and how the combination of works become related – sometimes simply due to the fact that they are installed next to each other. This is one of the things we've learned from the recent development of curated group exhibitions, and something that can be taken advantage of so that individual artists may be liberated from the feeling of obligation that an exhibition has to be consistent in presenting a singular vision or producing a unified effect.

In each other's presence, the two types of work Antezzo presented in Göttingen – the early narrative-driven pieces and the later abstract works – offer the opportunity to consider this play of different types of information against each other. The exhibition becomes a conversation where information is a formal quality as much as a narrative. Here intertextuality and threads of information function as a way of facilitating experience while not necessarily providing factual nuggets or anything to be used for practical purposes. Perhaps the meaning lies less in any use value and more in the continuous activity of the acquisition of expanded understanding. And if this all sounds a little psychedelic, maybe it is.

The "meaning of presence" was the lesson taught by Minimal art; works that, according to Michael Fried, made up the "theatrical" "silent presence of another person". Perhaps the inversion of this, the presence of meaning, could now be equally interesting. It's possible that various kinds of information could create an atmosphere of meaning, even when the sum total of this meaning isn't immediately available or even entirely clear. Maybe the simple act of being in or moving through the presence of such a framework of meaning could be sufficient in terms of whatever personal insight each spectator might happen to reach. Ultimately, this will lead to accusations of "aestheticism" and of stripping art of its "critical potential". This criticism, of course, is based on very particular ideas about what knowledge and understanding really is. It also has a tendency to plunge, accidentally or by design, into exactly the kind of transcendentalism it's trying to expose.

A piece like *No one is born, No one dies, No one comes, No one goes* (2005) could be understood as a transitional piece that bridges the earlier and later works in the exhibition. The imagery of the work is simple: it shows one iteration of the phase of the moon. The title of the work is clearly Hindu in spirit, but also modernist – the second half being identical with Beckett where, "no one comes, no one goes" is followed by "…it's terrible". This would be the favored reading today, Modernism being a more palatable frame of reference than an Eastern religion. (Or maybe not.)

European producers of luxury watches have long known that for the Asian market watches that include the moon phase complication are much more in demand than they are in Europe. In contrast, the phase of the moon, and the moon in general, might be a hard sell as relevant imagery for an American artist living in Berlin today. Our immediate connotations are, at best, various streams of feminist art of the kind Lucy Lippard outlined in *Overlay – Contemporary Art and the Art of Prehistory* (1983), in which ancient works that often deal with cyclical phenomena were attributed to recent art practices that were predominantly feminist in nature. To return to the split relevance of Beckett and Hindu philosophy, however, the paradox of time passing is of course that it is always both soothing and terrible. This relatively banal truth (in the sense that every paradox is a well-formulated self-evident truth) simply invites us to make a choice between ways we want to approach it. It's *the* basic, prosaic, existential choice.

While few would claim that contemporary artists have a limited pool of imagery and content available to them, post-modern image selection nevertheless tends to be sourced from history, news, popular culture, or the art world itself. This, of course, is what a lot of Antezzo's earlier work does as well. The recent abstract works are thematically removed from the earlier use of published images and stories that Antezzo has researched, and represent different, additional interests. Iconoclastic tendencies are an interesting, shared feature of Semitic art and early Modernism. Geometry, symmetrical patterns and abstract patterns have always been closely related to mystical, religious, or spiritual insight, throughout the history of visual art. Western conceptual artists, however, were inspired more by the creative desire to avoid intention and by how the use of symmetrical patterns – such as the grid – in that sense served a pragmatic, art-specific function as painterly ready-mades. Early modernist abstraction, however, was always intimately involved with the desire for more basic truths, in the sense parodied by Bruce Nauman in his *The True Artist Helps The World by Revealing Mystic Truths* (1967).

In Antezzo's case the abstract works appear more like improvisations – quick, almost sketch-like if it weren't for the fact that they're already so formally tight. This is true both with regard to the drawings and the closely related string works, which in a sense also offer a bridge between the tapestry works and the later drawings. They look like technical drawings, or scientific material that's been copied or used as inspiration. Another aspect to these works is the quickness with which they're made and seen. Their speed makes them altogether more suitable to being understood as having been created almost as abstract snapshots, but also as something you can zap through like you would a selection of television shows: quickly drawn and quickly consumed. Normally symmetrical works seem to invite prolonged, deep concentration. Dan Flavin famously didn't want people to treat his works as environments, but as installations that the visitor should walk in, look at, and then leave. The abstract works in the exhibition seem to function in a very similar way. It's possible to ponder them, of course, but the combinations of shapes and colors are most enjoyable when we pass through them quickly, walking back and forth, glancing at them, yet also taking them in slowly, even subconsciously. Under more alert scrutiny they might reveal something, but knowing that they're not obliged to, they instead become more alluring since they're not really supposed to be "read". Instead they form, simply (not merely), another presence; something that occupies the space with us. This makes them somehow more sympathetic, insofar as they do not make the usual demands to connect the dots, to penetrate the works, and track down what their references are, or what they might mean. That is why it's interesting to have them presented alongside older works; works that to a much larger degree do make such demands. This, ultimately, means that the abstract works simply ask us to connect a different set of dots.

The overall structure of the exhibition – its combination of older and newer works, and the very different qualities of these works – could lead us down two different paths. We either attempt to find similar kinds of meaning in all the works, or we adopt the approach that the older works might be released from some of their original duties, through the hindsight of the more open, perhaps empty, recent works. This does not involve anything becoming meaningless, but it does involve dealing with another kind of meaning altogether, one that is closer in spirit to the meaning of presence that has always been the dominant feature of non-representational art.

John Dewey wrote, in *Art as Experience* (1934), about "the organization of energies" and the rhythm of constructed relationships. Any exhibition is an example of how "the structure of the object is such that its force interacts happily (but not easily) with the energies that issue from the experience itself; when their mutual affinities and antagonisms work together to bring about a substance that develops cumulatively and surely (but not too steadily) toward a fulfilling of impulsions."

The combination of works at play here and the narrative created throughout more than twenty years of practice goes about presenting itself in such a way. There are affinities between the abstract drawings and the works that use historical material to explore questions about the relationships between history, power, and representation. The way in which these simultaneously engage offers no immediately available representation of content, and in the end this becomes the real story of how these works – together – form a springboard for individual experiences and readings.

Erlend Hammer

16. *No One is Born, No One Dies, No One Comes, No One Goes,*
    2005, oil on linen, eight elements, 50 x 70 cm ea.

WORKS IN EXHIBITIONS AND LIST OF ILLUSTRATION

Numbers indicate artworks in the exhibition, fig. indicate illustrations.

1. *Gruppe von zwölf*,
   2008-2010 casein on paper, table and glass,
   Courtesy Klosterfelde, Berlin
2. *Gruppe von dreizehn*,
   2008-2010 casein on paper, table and glass,
   Courtesy Klosterfelde, Berlin
3. *Group of fünfzehn*,
   2008-2010 casein on paper, table and glass,
   Courtesy Klosterfelde, Berlin

4. *Evening news. Alan Turing. The enigma*, 2002, pencil and graphite on paper, diptych, 23 x 30.5 cm,
   Courtesy Klosterfelde, Berlin
5. *T.I.M*, 2008, gouache on cotton twill, 40 x 40 cm,
   Courtesy Klosterfelde, Berlin

fig aa. TIM, calculating machine,
         Ludwig Spitz, GmbH Berlin, 1907
fig ab. Enigma Cipher machine, Germany 1920s
fig ac. *alanturing.org*, 1999,
         oil on linen, 107 x 61 cm, private collection, USA
fig ad. Bombe, Cryptanalysis device built in Bletchley Park by the British in 1939, designed by Alan Turing.
fig ae. David Hilbert, 1862-1943: one of the most influential Mathematicians of the 20th century.

6. *History of Computing*, home.t-online.de/home/horst.zuse/show.html (Konrad Zuse), 1999, oil on canvas, diptych, 76 x 61cm and 16 x 82.5 cm, Courtesy Klosterfelde, Berlin

fig ba. Z1 computer, built in Konrad Zuse's parents' living room, Berlin, 1941.
fig bb. Logo of Zuse computer firm.
fig bc. Young Konrad Zuse at work in his workshop c. 1941
fig bd. Zuse with model of windmill tower of his design c. 1990
fig be. Programs for Zuse's Z4 computer were loaded on recycled film stock.

7. *Bell Labs II*, 1999, oil on linen, diptych, 91 x 152 cm,
   Courtesy Klosterfelde, Berlin

fig ca. Family with console radio, c. 1950
fig cb. Paravox Model K transistor hearing aid, 1953
fig cc. Ipod shuffle, 2010
fig cd. http://www.emsp.tu-berlin.de/lehre/mixed-signal-baugruppen/
fig ce. 1956, radios: Neiman-Marcus advertisement, price: $56

fig cf. 1956, Felker and Harris program TRADIC, AT&T Bell Laboratories' first fully transistorized computer. It contained nearly 800 transistors instead of vacuum tubes. Transistors — completely cold, highly efficient amplifying devices invented at Bell Labs — enabled the machine to operate on less than 100 watts, or one-twentieth the power required by comparable vacuum tube computers. The computer occupied only 3 cubic feet
fig cg. Martin Cooper, inventor of the cell phone.
fig ch. image source: http://www.ehow.com/video_5112666_miniaturization-computer-technology_.html

8. *Nam June Paik, Video Time - Video Space* (Edition Cantz, 1991), p.31, 1997, oil on linen, diptych, 107 x 71 cm
   private collection, Berlin

fig da. Nam June Paik, Magnet TV, 1965.jpg
         image source: https://pacer.ischool.utexas.edu/handle/2081/9110?mode=full
fig db. Sony portapak video system,
fig dc. Nam June Paik, *TV Buddha*, 1974, closed circuit video installation with bronze sculpture

fig ea. *Web of anxiety*, 1991
9. *Deep Cover*, 1991, acrylic on canvas, 122 x 92 cm
fig eb. *A.T.P.M., 1968-75*, 1990, acrylic on canvas, 122 x 91 cm
fig ec. *A Friend of the Chinese People*, 1990, acrylic on canvas, 61 x 91 cm
fig ed. *Now, more than Ever*, 1991, acrylic on canvas, 30 x 40 cm, Private collection New York
fig ef. *Being 2*, 1991, acrylic on canvas, 46 x 61 cm

fig eg   *M.O.T.W*, (corner), 1990, acrylic on canvas, 61 x 61 cm
fig eh. *M.O.T.W*, (box), 1990, acrylic on canvas, 61 x 61 cm
fig ef. *M.O.T.W*, 1990, acrylic on canvas, 100 x 140 cm

10. *Mr. Fuller*, 1999, oil on linen, diptych

11. *Sechs auf dem Wall*,
    2010, cotton knitting wool, dimensions variable

fig fa. *Multiplexing Array for Clocking*,
         2008, gouache and acrylic on canvas, 60 x 120 cm
fig fb. *Forrest Mimms III*, (sound synthesiser),
         2008, gouache and acrylic on canvas, 120 x 80 cm

fig fc.   *Irrational clock*,
          2008, microprocessor, components and software,
          dimensions variable
fig fd.   *Fuzz Face*,
          2008 gouache on paper, 15 x 22 cm
fig fe.   *double numbers*,
          2008, gouache on cotton twill, 40 x 50 cm
   12.   *untitled*, 2009, casein on canvas 40 x 40 cm

fig ga.   U.S. Postage stamp honoring R. Buckminster Fuller, 2004
          image source: http://www.usps.com/communications
          /news/stamps/2004/sr04_043.htm
fig gb.   Tensegrity model, R. Buckminster Fuller Papers
          image source: http://www.oac.cdlib.org
          /ark:/13030/kt0s2002kt/?docId=
          kt0s2002kt&brand=oac4&layout=printable-details
fig gc.   Model from Göttingener Sammlung Mathematischer
          Modelle (Goettingen Mathematical model collection)
          founded by Hermann Amandus Schwarz and Felix Klein.
          Cubic ellipse (red) as a section of a circular cone (yellow)
          and a circular cylinder (blue) with a common generatrix
          (green). Threads in wooden frame
          image source: http://intranet.uni-math.gwdg.de
          /modellsammlung/
fig gd.   *Untitled*,
          2007, 30 x 42 cm, color aid paper collage,
          private collection, Berlin
fig ge.   Installation view, Schuster residence, Strelitzerstr., Berlin,
          PMW Exhibition, 2007,
          5 point figure, string & masking tape, 2007
fig gf   *Installation*, Klosterfelde, Berlin, 2009
fig gg   *vier, sechs, sieben K und die verbotenen Minoren*,
          2009, mauerschnur (bricklayer cord), dimensions variable
          installation with Elise Florenty (wooden numbers)
          Künstlerhäuser Worpswede / Barkenhoff-Stiftung,
fig gh   *11/12, 13/14,* installation, Klosterfelde Berlin,
          2009, colored cord over painted wall, 362 x 178 cm

fig ha   www.ezln.org.mx,
          2002, Tapestry, Haute Lisse, handwoven wool tapestry,
          Taller Mexicano de Gobelinos, Guadalajara,
          210 x 190 cm, Abraham Flores, Weaver
   13.   *Zukunft Titel*,
          2010, Tapestry, Haute Lisse, handwoven wool tapestry,
          Taller Mexicano de Gobelinos, Guadalajara,
          195 x 200 cm, Antonio Flores, Weaver,
          Courtesy Arena Mexico, Guadalajara

fig hb.   Wool hanging to dry on the roof of the factory.
fig hc.   Threads from the color room, TMdG.
fig hd.   Sr. Rafael Morquecho dying raw wool.
fig he.   Tapestry *Hermano Vianna*, in progress
fig hf.   *Hermano Vianna*,
          2003, Haute Lisse, handwoven wool tapestry,
          320 x 250 cm, Abraham Flores, Weaver,
          Courtesy Arena Mexico, Guadalajara
fig hg.   Preparing the Tapestry for sewing process on,
          HRH Sultan bin Abdul Aziz Al Saud,
          2003, Haute Lisse, handwoven wool tapestry,
          320 x 250 cm, Manuel Diaz., Weaver,
          Courtesy Arena Mexico, Guadalajara
fig hi.   Installation view, *In attesa di Risposta*,
          Supportico Lopez, Napoli, 2007

   14.   *Untitled*,
          2009, casein on canvas, 40 x 40 cm
          Courtesy Klosterfelde, Berlin
   15.   *Tom Watson, (Think)*,
          1999-2000, oil on linen, diptych, 173 x 203 cm
          Courtesy Klosterfelde, Berlin

fig ia   CPLY, *Think*, 1972, polyester flag.
fig ib.   A. Kaprow, Assemblage, Environments & Happenings
          (New York, N.D.), p. 326,
          1995, oil on linen, diptych, 76 x 163 cm, private collection
fig ic.   Charles Demuth, *love, love, love (homage to Gertrude Stein)*
          oil on board, c. 1928. 50 x 60 cm
fig id.   *Altrove*,
          2008, oil on linen, 70 x 100 cm
fig ie.   *Spirit*,
          1991, acrylic on canvas, 76 x 76 cm
fig if.   Thomas Watson in his office at IBM.

   39.   *No One Is Born, No One Dies,*
          No One Comes, No One Goes,
          2005, oil on linen (eight elements), 50 x 70 cm, ea.
          Courtesy Klosterfelde, Berlin

WORKS IN EXHIBITION NOT ILLUSTRATED

   41.   *Vier an der Wand*,
          2010, cotton knitting wool, dimensions variable
   41.   *Vier, Sechs, Sieben*,
          2009, mixed media, 50 x 100 cm,
          Collection Barkenhoff-Stiftung, Worpswede

SOLO EXHIBITIONS / SELECTED

2010   *Gedankenstriche*, Kunstverein Göttingen, with Elise Florenty, (cat.), Göttingen, D

2009   Silberraum, Die Schute, Hamburg, D

2006   *Sun In My Hands*, Klosterfelde, Berlin, D

2005   Michele Maccarone Inc, NYC, USA
Ex post Facto, Galerie GP & N Vallois, Paris, F

2003   Sprüth Magers Projekte, Munich, D
Arena Mexico, Guadalajara, MX

2002   *http://matthew.antezzo.org/links*, Klosterfelde, Berlin, D

2001   Eleni Koroneou Gallery, Athens, GR

2000   Blum & Poe, Santa Monica, USA

1999   *Spy versus Spy*, Klosterfelde, Berlin, D
Forum for Contemporary Art, St. Louis, USA

1998   Basilico Fine Arts, (cat.), NYC, USA
Klosterfelde (Statement Art Basel), Berlin, D

1997   Mario Diacono Gallery, Boston, USA
Le Case d'Arte, Milan, I
Klosterfelde, (cat.), Berlin, D

1996   Klosterfelde, Berlin, D
Basilico Fine Arts, NYC, USA
Galerie Philomene Magers, Cologne, D

1995   Gian Enzo Sperone, Rome, I
Galerie Georges-Philippe Vallois, Paris, F

1994   Interim Art, London, GB
Basilico Fine Arts, NYC, USA

1993   Basilico Fine Arts, NYC, USA
Galerie Georges Philippe Vallois, (cat.), Paris, F

1991   Randy Alexander, NYC, USA
Galerie Georges Philippe Vallois, Paris, F

GROUP EXHIBITIONS / SELECTED

2009   *Exchanging Insights - A Temporary Art Project At the Residence of the U.S. Ambassador to Germany,* December 10, 2009 - Spring 2010
Portrait of the Artist as a Biker, Olivier Mosset, Le Magasin, CRAC Grenoble, F
Wright, Klosterfelde, Linienstrasse 160, Berlin, D
Unerreichbar ist gerade nah genug, Galerie Alexandra Saheb, Berlin, D

2008   *Exploring surrealism*, Rose Art Museum, Waltham, MA, USA
remixed, Galerie Alexandra Saheb, Berlin, D
Moralische Fantasien – Künstlerische Strategien in Zusammenhang mit der Klimaerwärmung, Kunstmuseum des Kantons Thurgau, Kartause (cat.), Ittingen, CH
Freunde und Bekannte, Sparwasser, Berlin, D
Faces, Eleni Koroneou, Athens, GR

2007   *In Attesa di Risposta*, Supportico Lopez, Naples, I
Historyteller. Curated by Raimar Stange, Galerie Lautom, Oslo, NO
REF. curated by Gigiotto Del Vecchio, 1/9, unosunove arte contemporanea, Rome, I
The Re-Distribution of the Sensible, Magnus Müller, Berlin, D
Very Abstract Hyper Figurative, curated by Jens Hoffmann, Thomas Dane Gallery, (cat.), London, GB
Full House – Malerei aus der Sammlung Falckenberg, Overbeck Gesellschaft, Lübeck, D
The Evil: Teil 1: Presse & Politik, curated by Raimar Stange, Galerie Gebr. Lehmann, (cat.), Dresden, D

2006   *Down By Law*, 2006 Whitney Biennial, Whitney Museum of American Art, (cat.), NYC, USA
Tropicália: A Revolution in Brazilian Culture, (cat.), BXMA, Bronx, NYC, USA
Museum of Contemporary Art, Chicago, USA,
Barbican Gallery, London, GB,
Haus der Kulturen der Welt, Berlin, D

2005   Museum of Contemporary Art, Chicago, USA

2004   *Common Property / Allgemeingut, 6. Werkleitz Biennale*, Volkspark, Halle (Saale), D

Reanimation, Kunstmuseum Thun, (cat.),Thun, CH
Arbeiten auf Papier / Works on paper,
Sprüth Magers Projekte, Munich, D
Likeness, CCAC Wattis Institute for Contemporary Arts, curated by Matthew Higgs,
(cat.), San Francisco, USA

2003 *Living with Duchamp*, The Tang Teaching Museum and Art Gallery at Skidmore College, Saratoga Springs, NY, USA.
Influence, Anxiety, and Gratitude,
curated by Bill Arning, MIT List
Visual Arts Center, Cambridge, USA

2001 *Drawings*, sommer contemporary art, Tel Aviv, IL

2000 *superpredators*, CRP gallery, NYC, USA
PICT, Walter Phillips Gallery at The Banff Centre, curated by Yvonne Force & Carmen Zita, Alberta, CA

1999 *artLovers*, curated by Márcia Fortes, TRACEY- Liverpool Biennial of Contemporary Art, GB
Malerei, INIT Kunst-Halle Berlin, D
Blum and Poe, Santa Monica, USA
Nach-Bild, Kunsthalle Basel,(cat.), Basel, CH
Attitudes, *Autour de R2 / 12*, Geneva, CH
Charim Klocker, Vienna, A
Eleni Koroneou Gallery, Athens, GR

1998 *Surfacing, Contemporary Drawing*,
ICA, London, GB
I Love New York, Edinburgh International Arts Festival, Edinburgh College of Art, GB

1997 *Project Painting*, Basilico Fine Arts & Lehmann Maupin, NYC, USA
Art on Paper, Weatherspoon Art Gallery, University of North Carolina,(cat.),
Greensboro, USA

1996 *100 Photographs*, American Fine Arts, NYC, USA
Two Girls on the Beach...2, Galerie Declercq, Knokke-Heist, B
Wish You Were Here, De Appel, Amsterdam, NL
Centro Figura, Studio Guenzani, Milan, I

Centro Figura, La Galleria d'Art Moderna e Contemporanea e Pinacoteca Nazionale, Cesena, I
Everything is Real, Jessica Fredericks Gallery, NYC, USA
The Power of Suggestion: Narrative and Notation in Contemporary Drawing,
curated by Connie Butler, MOCA,
(cat.), Los Angeles, USA
Painting into Photography/Photography into Painting, Museum of Contemporary Art,
(cat.), Miami, USA

1995 *Pittura Immedia*, Mücsarnok, Budapest, H
Summer Fling, Basilico Fine Arts, NYC, USA
Pittura Immedia, Neue Galerie am Landesmuseum, (cat.), Graz, A

1994 *Pieces à Conviction*, FRAC, Languedoc- Roussillon, F
When Attitudes Become Form, Montclair Art Museum, NJ, USA
Crash, Thread Waxing Space, (cat.), NYC, USA
SP-NY, Galeria Camargo Vilaca,
(cat.), Sao Paolo, BR
Backstage, Kunstmuseum Luzern, (cat.), CH
Desire and Loss, Carl Solway Gallery, Cincinatti, USA
Out West and Back East, Santa Monica, USA

1993 *The Figure as Fiction*, The Contemporary Arts Center, (cat.), Cincinatti, USA
ghost-limb, Basilico Fine Arts, NYC, USA
Backstage, curated by Stephan Schmidt-Wullfen, Kunstverein, (cat.), Hamburg, D
Andrea Rosen Gallery, NYC, USA

1991 John Post Lee Gallery, NYC, USA
Home for Contemporary Theater and Art, NYC, USA
Exhibition Inaugurale, Maison Bellevue, Normandie, F

1990 Galerie Georges Philippe Vallois, Paris, F

1989 American Fine Arts, NYC, USA

This book was published on the occasion of the exhibition:
Gedankenstriche, Elise Florenty and Matthew Antezzo
Kunstverein Göttingen, March 28 - May 9, 2010

Editor: Bernd Milla, Kunstverein Göttingen, e.V.

Art direction and design: Livia Polidoro

Production coordination: Annette Thomas

Preproduction: Marianne Buchwalder

Copyediting: Anna Canby Monk

Reproductions: Oren Slor, Nick Ash, Thomas Jacobs,
Peter Muscato, Fred Scruton, Chip DiPippo
Photo: Peter Heller (cover, p. 4, 17)

Printed by Agit-Druck GmbH

© 2010 for the reproduced works the artist

© 2010 argobooks and the authors

Thanks to,

Yumi Tanabe, Jaime Ashida, Martin Klosterfelde, Johannes Kiessler,
Vincent J. Antezzo, Alfons Klosterfelde, Erlend Hammer, Lena
Kiessler, Katharina Garrelt, Sil Egger, Raimar Stange, Renata
Trejo, Dennis Schroer, Stefan Schuster, Elise Florenty, Mark Räder,
Professor Simon Patterson, Nick Loessing, Adriana Salazar Arroyo,
Nick Ash, Martin Bauer, Mai Hofsted Gunnes, John Beek, Helmut
Wenzel, Hanjo Rhee, Harry Siegloch, Jennifer Allen, Michael Baers,
Anke Bräuler, Julia Wachtel, Mia Antezzo, Matthew R. Antezzo,
everyone at Künstlerhäuser Worpswede & the Barkenhoff-Stiftung,
and finally, also to the manager, the producer and the Princess.

questions or comments: antezzoberlin@gmail.com

Published by

 argobooks

Choriner Straße 57
10435 Berlin
Germany

Tel. +49 30 41725631
www.argobooks.de

ISBN: 978-3-941560-72-7

Printed in Germany

KLOSTERFELDE

kunstvereingöttingen e.V.
mit artothek